# What Do Babies Do in Heaven?

Written by Sheba Williams
Illustrated by Ananta Mohanta

Archway Publishing books may be ordered through booksellers or by contacting:

Archway Publishing
1663 Liberty Drive
Bloomington, IN 47403
www.archwaypublishing.com
844-669-3957

Because of the dynamic nature of the Internet, any web addresses or links contained in this book may have changed since publication and may no longer be valid. The views expressed in this work are solely those of the author and do not necessarily reflect the views of the publisher, and the publisher hereby disclaims any responsibility for them.

Any people depicted in stock imagery provided by Getty Images are models, and such images are being used for illustrative purposes only.
Certain stock imagery © Getty Images.

ISBN: 978-1-6657-4923-7 (hc)
ISBN: 978-1-6657-4820-9 (sc)
ISBN: 978-1-6657-4819-3 (e)

Print information available on the last page.

Archway Publishing rev. date: 09/07/2023

For Justice Anais Williams and for babies that were born straight into Heaven or stayed only a short while on Earth

"I knew you before I formed you in your mother's womb. Before you were born I set you apart ..." (Jer. 1:5 New Living Translation)

What do babies do in Heaven? Oh, wouldn't you like to know? Because babies are such blessings, and Heaven is so very magical!

Do babies giggle way up in Heaven? Do they babble? Do they coo? And if they giggle way up in Heaven, do their bright eyes light up too?

Are babies deemed angels upon arrival without any tasks to fulfill or try? If so, are their angel wings really heavy or light and perfectly baby-sized?

Could those angel wings be fluffy or silky like feathers on delicate skin? Are the angel wings adorable and small or big enough to wrap up in?

What do babies do in Heaven? Do they play with joyful little baby friends? Do babies meet and greet each other with wet smiles and baby grins?

Are some babies fortunate to arrive together with familiar and treasured friends because they weren't alone in mommy's belly? Are there multiples? Are there twins?

Do babies play popular games in Heaven like Pat-a-Cake and Peek-a-Boo, or do they only play Heavenly games?  Oh, don't you wish you had a clue?

Since the kingdom of God belongs to such babies,
are boys honored with morning skies so blue?
Then, when the sun is setting, and the skies turn
pink, is this in honor of our baby girls, too?

Is there a need for baby diapers?  Are
babies adorned with precious jewels?
Is there a need for baby bibs in Heaven
to catch their endless baby drool?

Do babies smell of baby lotion or maybe a sweet, heavenly perfume? Do they splash around on rain clouds? Do they laugh when thunder booms?

Do babies crawl around in Heaven?
Do they rest peacefully amongst the
clouds? Do they raise their arms and
arch their backs to stretch? Such a sight
would make the whole world smile!

If it's ever warm in Heaven, do babies get bright red, rosy cheeks? When babies discover their baby parts, do they suck their toes and nibble on their feet?

Just what do babies do in Heaven? Do they watch over their families? Do they send sweet kisses in the wind to their mommies and daddies? Do they send signs that they are near like butterflies passing through or feathers from their angel wings that the wind carries straight to you?

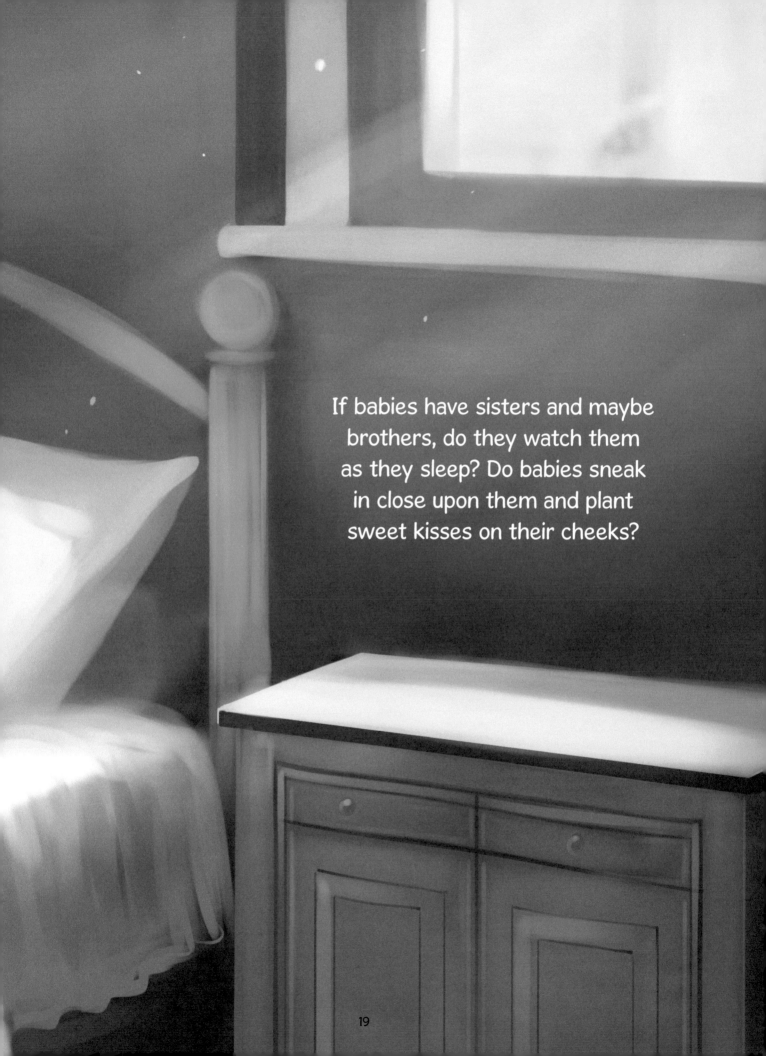

If babies have sisters and maybe
brothers, do they watch them
as they sleep? Do babies sneak
in close upon them and plant
sweet kisses on their cheeks?

What do babies do in Heaven? Only one thing is for sure. Babies are safe in the Kingdom of God waiting to reunite with loved ones and live forevermore.

# Author Biography

Sheba Williams resides in Louisiana with her husband and three children. She began a career working with children and families in 2008 after earning a Bachelor's degree in Psychology from the University of Louisiana at Lafayette. Sheba went on to obtain a Master's degree in Social Work from Louisiana State University in 2015 which she uses to serve vulnerable populations in her community. During her career of helping others navigate through difficulties in life, Sheba and her husband experienced miscarriage in 2012 and stillbirth in 2016. Those experiences of loss motivated Sheba to create a book dedicated to both loss and hope as a reminder to families everywhere all is not lost in loss.

Printed in the United States
by Baker & Taylor Publisher Services